TALKING

LIKE THE RAIN

TALKING LIKE

A Read-to-me Book of Poems

Selected by X. J. Kennedy and Dorothy M. Kennedy

Little, Brown and Company
Boston New York London

THE RAIN

Illustrated by Jane Dyer

For Kate, Dave, Matthew, Dan, and Josh,
with happy memories
X.J.K. and D.M.K.

For Maria
J.D.

First Paperback Edition

Acknowledgments of permission to reprint previously
published material appear on page 95.

Library of Congress Cataloging-in-Publication Data

Kennedy, X. J.
Talking like the rain: a read-to-me book of poems/
by X. J. Kennedy and Dorothy M. Kennedy; illustrated by Jane Dyer.
p.   cm.
Summary: An illustrated collection of poems for very young children,
including works by Robert Louis Stevenson, Edward Lear,
and Jack Prelutsky.
ISBN 0-316-48889-5 (hc)/ISBN 0-316-38491-7 (pb)
1. Children's poetry.   [1. Poetry — Collections.]
I. Kennedy, Dorothy M. (Dorothy Mintzlaff)
II. Dyer, Jane, ill.   III. Title.
PN6109.97.K46   1991
821.008'09282 — dc20
89-13504

HC: 20 19 18 17 16 15 14 13 12
PB: 10 9 8 7 6 5 4 3 2 1

IM

Printed in China

Illustrations done in Winsor and Newton watercolors on Waterford
140-pound hot press paper.

One evening out in the maize-field, where we had been harvesting maize, breaking off the cobs and throwing them on to the ox-carts, to amuse myself, I spoke to the field labourers, who were mostly quite young, in Swaheli verse. There was no sense in the verse, it was made for the sake of the rhyme. . . .

It caught the interest of the boys, they formed a ring around me. They . . . waited eagerly for the rhyme, and laughed at it when it came. I tried to make them themselves find the rhyme and finish the poem when I had begun it, but they could not, or would not, do that, and turned away their heads. As they had become used to the idea of poetry, they begged: "Speak again. Speak like rain." Why they should feel verse to be like rain I do not know. It must have been, however, an expression of applause, since in Africa rain is always longed for and welcomed.

— Isak Dinesen, *Out of Africa*

CONTENTS

PLAY

FAMILIES

JUST FOR FUN

BIRDS, BUGS, AND BEASTS

RHYMES AND SONGS

MAGIC AND WONDER

WIND AND WEATHER

CALENDARS AND CLOCKS

DAY AND NIGHT

LITTLE SONG

Carmencita loves Patrick.
Patrick loves Si Lan Chen.
Xenophon loves Mary Jane.
Hildegarde loves Ben.

Lucienne loves Eric.
Giovanni loves Emma Lee.
Natasha loves Miguelito —
And Miguelito loves me.

Ring around the Maypole!
Ring around we go —
Weaving our bright ribbons
Into a rainbow!

Langston Hughes

PLAY

GETTING DIRTY

Let's go rolling, rolling
Fast as round rocks roll
Down a hillside, hollering
When we hit a hole.

Make believe we're rabbits
In a garden patch —
Quick lips clipping lettuce leaves,
Fast feet dogs can't catch.

Let's play knights in armor,
Bashing swords in battle,
Shake a stone inside a can,
Make a thunder rattle.

Let's play I'm a tiger.
You yell *Help! I'm bit!*
Let's not play that anymore —
Tag! You're IT!

Here's a peaceful puddle,
Just the thing to smash.
What a mess of mushy mud!
In and out we splash.

How will Mother wash us off?
Mother only knows —
Line us up against the house,
Slosh us with a hose.

Dorthi Charles

WHAT JOHNNY TOLD ME

I went to play with Billy. He
Threw my cap into a tree.
I threw his glasses in the ditch.
He dipped my shirt in a bucket of pitch.
I hid his shoes in the garbage can.
And then we heard the ice cream man.
So I bought him a cone. He bought me one.
A true good friend is a lot of fun!

John Ciardi

THE NEW LITTLE BOY

A new little boy moved in next door
So I climbed a tree and bounced on a limb
And asked where he used to live before
And he didn't know but his name was Tim,
So I told all three of my names to him.

When he didn't say anything after that
I hung by my knees to see if he scared
And meowed and made my face like a cat,
But he only stood in his yard and stared,
He only watched like he never cared.

Well, all I know is his name is Tim
And I don't think very much of him.

Harry Behn

WHERE GO THE BOATS?

Dark brown is the river,
    Golden is the sand.
It flows along for ever,
    With trees on either hand.

Green leaves a-floating,
    Castles of the foam,
Boats of mine a-boating —
    Where will all come home?

On goes the river
    And out past the mill,
Away down the valley,
    Away down the hill.

Away down the river,
    A hundred miles or more,
Other little children
    Shall bring my boats ashore.

Robert Louis Stevenson

KICK A LITTLE STONE

When you are walking by yourself
Here's something nice to do:
Kick a little stone and watch it
Hop ahead of you.

The little stone is round and white,
Its shadow round and blue.
Along the sidewalk over the cracks
The shadow bounces too.

Dorothy Aldis

AT THE SEASIDE

When I was down beside the sea,
A wooden spade they gave to me
To dig the sandy shore.

My holes were hollow like a cup,
In every hole the sea came up,
Till it could hold no more.

Robert Louis Stevenson

A SWING SONG

    Swing, swing,
    Sing, sing
Here's my throne, and I am a King!
    Swing, sing,
    Swing, sing,
Farewell earth, for I'm on the wing!

    Low, high,
    Here I fly,
Like a bird through sunny sky;
    Free, free
    Over the lea,
Over the mountain, over the sea!

    Up, down,
    Up and down,
Which is the way to London Town?
    Where, where?
    Up in the air,
Close your eyes, and now you are there!

    Soon, soon
    Afternoon,
Over the sunset, over the moon;
    Far, far
    Over all bar,
Sweeping on from star to star!

    No, no,
    Low, low,
Sweeping daisies with my toe.
    Slow, slow,
    To and fro,
Slow —
    slow —
       slow —
          slow.

William Allingham

THE SWING

How do you like to go up in a swing,
    Up in the air so blue?
Oh, I do think it the pleasantest thing
    Ever a child can do!

Up in the air and over the wall,
    Till I can see so wide,
Rivers and trees and cattle and all
    Over the countryside —

Till I look down on the garden green,
    Down on the roof so brown —
Up in the air I go flying again,
    Up in the air and down!

Robert Louis Stevenson

AT THE PLAYGROUND

Away down deep and away up high,
a swing drops you into the sky.
Back, it draws you away down deep,
forth, it flings you in a sweep
all the way to the stars and back
— Goodby, Jill; Goodby, Jack:
shuddering climb wild and steep,
away up high, away down deep.

William Stafford

SOMETIMES

Sometimes
when I skip or hop
or when I'm
    jumping

Suddenly
I like to stop
and listen to me
    thumping.

Lilian Moore

LEMONADE STAND

Every summer
under the shade
we fix up a stand
to sell lemonade.

A stack of cups,
a pitcher of ice,
a shirtboard sign
to tell the price.

A dime for the big,
A nickel for small.
The nickel cup's short.
The dime cup's tall.

Plenty of sugar
to make it sweet,
and sometimes cookies
for us to eat.

But when the sun
moves into the shade
it gets too hot
to sell lemonade.

Nobody stops
so we put things away
and drink what's left
and start to play.

Myra Cohn Livingston

LEMONADE
5¢ small
10¢ large

17

THE ROSE ON MY CAKE

I went to a party,
A party for Pearly,
With presents and ice cream,
With favors and games.
I stayed very late
And I got there quite early.
I met all the guests
And I know all their names.
We sang and we jumped.
We jumped and we jostled.
We jostled and rustled
At musical chairs.
We ate up the cake
And we folded the candy in baskets
In napkins
We folded in squares.
We blew up balloons
And we danced without shoes.
We danced on the floor
And the rug and the bed.
We tripped and we trotted
In trios and twos.
And I neatly balanced myself
On my head.
Pearly just smiled
As she blew out the candles.
I gave the rose from my cake
To a friend,
Millicent Moss,
In her black patent sandals.
The trouble with parties is
All of them end.

Karla Kuskin

LET'S DRESS UP

Let's dress up in grown-up clothes:
    Swishing skirts
    That touch our toes;
    Wispy veils
    That hide our nose.
Let's dress up today.

    Feathered bonnet
    Trimmed with lace;
    Rouge and lipstick
    On our face;
    An umbrella
    (Just in case).
Let's dress up today.

Now we're ready.
Let's go walking
Down the street
(Pretend we're talking).
    Walking
    Talking
    Walking
    Talking,
All dressed up today.

Mary Ann Hoberman

THE LAND OF COUNTERPANE

When I was sick and lay a-bed,
I had two pillows at my head,
And all my toys beside me lay
To keep me happy all the day.

And sometimes for an hour or so
I watched my leaden soldiers go,
With different uniforms and drills,
Among the bed-clothes, through the hills.

And sometimes sent my ships in fleets
All up and down among the sheets;
Or brought my trees and houses out,
And planted cities all about.

I was the giant great and still
That sits upon the pillow-hill,
And sees before him dale and plain,
The pleasant Land of Counterpane.

Robert Louis Stevenson

FAMILIES

INVITATION

Listen! I've a big surprise!
My new mom has light-green eyes

and my new brother, almost ten,
is really smart. He helped me when

we did our homework. They moved in
a week ago. When we begin

to settle down, she said that you
could come for dinner. When you do

you'll like them, just like Dad and me,
so come and meet my family!

Myra Cohn Livingston

MY YELLOW STRAW HAT

Wearing my yellow straw hat
(Mama had just bought it),
I was going to see Aunt Bett
When a high wind caught it,

Took it up in the air
As I cried and watched it
Sailing high up there
Where I couldn't catch it,

Dropped it down in the ditch,
Where the water snatched it,
Made it tumble and pitch
Till the wetness had stretched it.

It was soggy and wet
When my aunt Bett found it.
She dried my yellow hat
And put a new ribbon 'round it.

Lessie Jones Little

LET'S BE MERRY

Mother shake the cherry-tree,
  Susan catch a cherry;
Oh how funny that will be,
  Let's be merry!

One for brother, one for sister,
  Two for mother more,
Six for father, hot and tired,
  Knocking at the door.

Christina Rossetti

PIGGY-BACK

My daddy rides me piggy-back.
My mama rides me, too.
But grandma says her poor old back
Has had enough to do.

Langston Hughes

DISOBEDIENCE

James James
Morrison Morrison
Weatherby George Dupree
Took great
Care of his Mother,
Though he was only three.
James James
Said to his Mother,
"Mother," he said, said he:
"You must never go down to the end of the town,
    if you don't go down with me."

James James
Morrison's Mother
Put on a golden gown,
James James
Morrison's Mother
Drove to the end of the town.
James James
Morrison's Mother
Said to herself, said she:
"I can get right down to the end of the town and be
    back in time for tea."

King John
Put up a notice,
"LOST or STOLEN or STRAYED!
JAMES JAMES
MORRISON'S MOTHER
SEEMS TO HAVE BEEN MISLAID.
LAST SEEN
WANDERING VAGUELY:
QUITE OF HER OWN ACCORD,
SHE TRIED TO GET DOWN TO THE END
    OF THE TOWN — FORTY SHILLINGS
    REWARD!"

James James
Morrison Morrison
(Commonly known as Jim)
Told his
Other relations
Not to go blaming *him*.
James James
Said to his Mother,
"Mother," he said, said he:
"You must *never* go down to the end of the town
  without consulting me."

James James
Morrison's mother
Hasn't been heard of since.
King John
Said he was sorry,
So did the Queen and Prince.
King John
(Somebody told me)
Said to a man he knew:
"If people go down to the end of the town, well, what
  can *anyone* do?"

(*Now then, very softly*)

J. J.
M. M.
W. G. Du P.
Took great
C/o his M*****
Though he was only 3.
J. J.
Said to his M*****
"M*****," he said, said he:
"You-must-never-go-down-to-the-end-of-the-town-
  if-you-don't-go-down-with ME!"

A. A. Milne

BILLY BATTER

Billy Batter,
What's the matter?
How come you're so sad?
I lost my cat
In the laundromat,
And a dragon ran off with my dad,
My dad—
A dragon ran off with my dad!

Billy Batter,
What's the matter?
How come you're so glum?
I ripped my jeans
On the Coke machine,
And a monster ran off with my mum,
My mum —
A monster ran off with my mum!

Billy Batter,
Now you're better —
Happy as a tack!
The dragon's gone
To Saskatchewan;
The monster fell
In a wishing-well;
The cat showed up
With a new-born pup;
I fixed the rips
With potato chips,
And my dad and my mum came back,
Came back —
My dad and my mum came back!

Dennis Lee

DOLL

The Christmas
when my sister came

she got a doll
without a name

and so I helped her out
and chose

Samantha

and put on her clothes
and dressed her up
and curled her hair.
I took Samantha everywhere

and hid her underneath the bed
so she could be my doll instead.

Myra Cohn Livingston

LATE FOR BREAKFAST

Who is it hides my sandals when I'm trying to get dressed?
And takes away the hairbrush that was lying on the chest?
I wanted to start breakfast before any of the others
But something's always missing or been borrowed by my brothers.
I think I'd better dress at night, and eat my breakfast too,
     Then when everybody's hurrying —
     I'll have nothing else to do.

Mary Dawson

WORKING WITH MOTHER

Some of the time
I get on the bus
with mother

(just the two of us)

and we go to the place
where she works all day.

We take some games
so I can play,

and some of the time
I help a lot
with work that mother

just forgot——
(or couldn't finish——
or did all wrong——)

It's good
she needs me
to come along.

Myra Cohn Livingston

I WOKE UP THIS MORNING

I woke up this morning
At quarter past seven.
I kicked up the covers
And stuck out my toe.
And ever since then
(That's a quarter past seven)
They haven't said anything
Other than "no."
They haven't said anything
Other than "Please, dear,
Don't do what you're doing,"
Or "Lower your voice."
Whatever I've done
And however I've chosen,
I've done the wrong thing
And I've made the wrong choice.
I didn't wash well
And I didn't say thank you.
I didn't shake hands
And I didn't say please.
I didn't say sorry
When passing the candy.
I banged the box into
Miss Witelson's knees.
I didn't say sorry.
I didn't stand straighter.
I didn't speak louder
When asked what I'd said.
Well, I said
That tomorrow
At quarter past seven
They can
Come in and get me.
I'm Staying In Bed.

Karla Kuskin

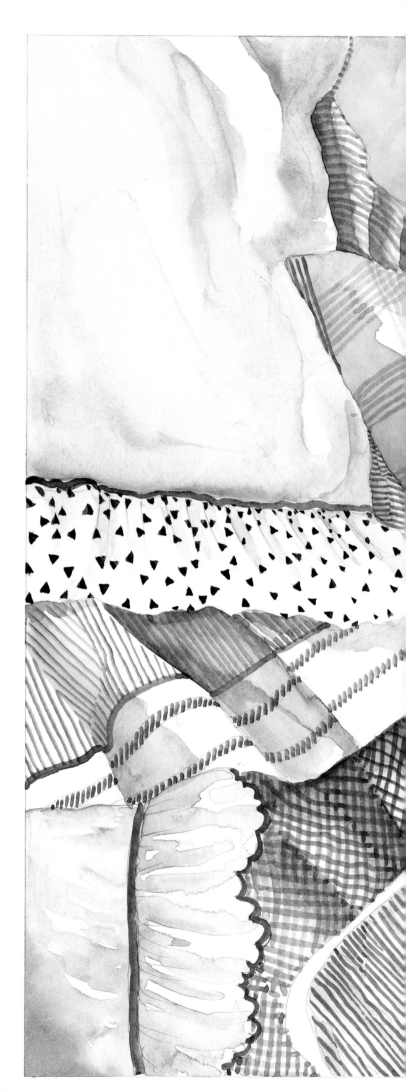

NIGHT FUN

I hear eating.
I hear drinking.
I hear music.
I hear laughter.
Fun is something
Grownups never have
Before my bedtime.
Only after.

Judith Viorst

BLANKET HOG

When my brother hogs
the blanket,
the only thing to do is
yank it.

Paul B. Janeczko

AROUND MY ROOM

I put on a pair of overshoes
And walk around my room,
With my Father's bamboo walking stick,
And my Mother's feather broom.

I walk and walk and walk and walk,
I walk and walk around.
I love my Father's tap-tap-tap,
My Mother's feathery sound.

William Jay Smith

JUST FOR FUN

AWAY DOWN EAST, AWAY DOWN WEST

Away down East, away down West,
Away down Alabama,
The only girl that I love best,
Her name is Susy Anna.

I took her to a ball one night
And sat her down to supper.
The table fell and she fell too
And stuck her nose in the butter,

The butter, the butter,
The holy margarine.
Two black eyes and a jelly nose
And all the rest painted green.

Anonymous
(*chanted by children in Edinburgh, Scotland*)

A PEANUT SAT ON A RAILROAD TRACK

A peanut sat on a railroad track,
His heart was all a-flutter;
The five-fifteen came rushing by —
Toot! Toot! Peanut butter!

Anonymous

HOW MUCH WOOD WOULD
A WOODCHUCK CHUCK?

How much wood would a woodchuck chuck
If a woodchuck could chuck wood?
He would chuck as much wood as a woodchuck would chuck,
If a woodchuck could chuck wood.

Anonymous

MY OLD HEN

I went down to my garden patch
To see if my old hen had hatched.
She'd hatched out her chickens and the peas were green.
She sat there a-pickin' on a tambourine.

Anonymous

THE PURPLE COW

I never saw a purple cow,
I never hope to see one;
But I can tell you, anyhow,
I'd rather see than be one!

Gelett Burgess

PAINTING THE GATE

I painted the mailbox. That was fun.
I painted it postal blue.
Then I painted the gate.
I painted a spider that got on the gate.
I painted his mate.
I painted the ivy around the gate.
Some stones I painted blue,
and part of the cat as he rubbed by.
I painted my hair. I painted my shoe.
I painted the slats, both front and back,
all their beveled edges, too.
I painted the numbers on the gate —
I shouldn't have, but it was too late.
I painted the posts, each side and top,
I painted the hinges, the handle, the lock,
several ants and a moth asleep in a crack.
At last I was through.
I'd painted the gate
shut, me out, with both hands dark blue,
as well as my nose, which,
early on, because of a sudden itch,
got painted. But wait!
I had painted the gate.

May Swenson

36

JOHN SMITH AND HIS SON, JOHN SMITH

John Smith and his son, John Smith,
    And his son's son John, and-a-one
    And-a-two and-a-three
And-a-rum-tum-tum, and-a
Lean John, and his son, lean John,
    And his lean son's John, and-a-one
    And-a-two and-a-three
And-a-drum-rum-rum, and-a
Rich John, and his son, rich John,
    And his rich son's John, and-a-one
    And-a-two and-a-three
And-a-pom-pom-pom, and-a-
Wise John, and his son, wise John,
    And his wise son's John, and-a-one
    And-a-two and-a-three
And-a-fee and-a-fee and-a-fee
    And-a-fee-fo-fum —
Voilà la vie, la vie, la vie,
    And-a-rummy-tummy-tum
    And-a-rummy-tummy-tum.

Wallace Stevens

MR. SLATTER

Ormsby Slatter
(crusty hatter)
made his hats
of brittle-batter.
These (as they
were most delicious,
scrumptious, and
indeed nutritious)
sold like hot cakes
through the town,
till the rain
came pouring down,
when they cried:
"Oh! Mister Slatter!
Dreadful and
deceitful hatter!
All your hats
have turned to mush."
Slatter said:
"Go home and wash!"

N. M. Bodecker

38

THERE WAS AN OLD WOMAN NAMED PIPER

There was an Old Woman named Piper
Who spoke like a windshield wiper.
    She would say: "Dumb Gump!
    Wet Stump! Wet Stump!"
And then like the voice of disaster
Her words would come faster and faster:
    "Dumb Gump! Dumb Gump!
    Wet Stump! Wet Stump!
    Wet Stump! Wet Stump!
    Tiddledy-diddledy-diddledy-bump . . .

    Bump . . .

      Bump . . .

        Bump . . .

          BUMP!"

— Which greatly annoyed *Mr.* Piper!

William Jay Smith

THERE WAS AN OLD MAN WITH A BEARD

There was an Old Man with a beard
Who said, "It is just as I feared! —
    Two Owls and a Hen,
    Four Larks and a Wren
Have all built their nests in my beard."

Edward Lear

THERE WAS A YOUNG LADY OF NIGER

There was a young lady of Niger
Who smiled as she rode on a Tiger;
 They came back from the ride
 With the lady inside,
And the smile on the face of the Tiger.

Anonymous

A MOUSE IN HER ROOM

A mouse in her room woke Miss Dowd.
She was frightened and screamed very loud.
Then a happy thought hit her —
To scare off the critter
She sat up in bed and meowed.

Anonymous

THE LION

Oh, weep for Mr. and Mrs. Bryan!
He was eaten by a lion;
Following which, the lion's lioness
Up and swallowed Bryan's Bryaness.

Ogden Nash

TUBE TIME

I turned on the TV
and what did I see?

I saw a can of cat food talking,
a tube of toothpaste walking.

>Peanuts, popcorn,
>cotton flannel,
>jump up, jump up,
>switch the channel.

I turned to station B
and what did I see?

I saw a shampoo bottle crying,
a pile of laundry flying.

>Peanuts, popcorn,
>cotton flannel,
>jump up, jump up,
>switch the channel.

I turned to station D
and what did I see?

I saw two spray cans warring,
a cup of coffee snoring.

>Peanuts, popcorn,
>cotton flannel,
>jump up, jump up,
>switch the channel.

I turned to station E
and what did I see?

I saw dancing fingers dialing,
an upset stomach smiling.

>Peanuts, popcorn,
>cotton flannelette,
>jump up, jump up,
>turn off the set.

Eve Merriam

MY TV CAME DOWN WITH A CHILL

My TV came down with a chill.
As soon as I saw it was ill
    I wrapped up its channels
    In warm winter flannels
And gave its antenna a pill.

Willard R. Espy

43

I EAT KIDS YUM YUM!

A child went out one day.
She only went to play.
A mighty monster came along
And sang its mighty monster song:

"I EAT KIDS YUM YUM!
I STUFF THEM DOWN MY TUM.
I ONLY LEAVE THE TEETH AND CLOTHES.
(I SPECIALLY LIKE THE TOES.)"

The child was not amused.
She stood there and refused.
Then with a skip and a little twirl
She sang the song of a hungry girl:

"I EAT MONSTERS BURP!
THEY MAKE ME SQUEAL AND SLURP.
IT'S TIME TO CHOMP AND TAKE A CHEW —
AND WHAT I'LL CHEW IS YOU!"

The monster ran like that!
It didn't stop to chat.
(The child went skipping home again
And ate her brother's model train.)

Dennis Lee

HURRY, HURRY, MARY DEAR!

Hurry, hurry, Mary dear,
fall is over, winter's here.

Not a moment to be lost,
in a minute we get frost!

In an hour we get snow!
Drifts like houses! Ten below!

Pick the apples, dill the pickles,
chop down trees for wooden nickels.

Dig the turnips, split the peas,
cook molasses, curdle cheese.

Churn the butter, smoke the hams,
can tomatoes, put up jams.

Stack the stove wood, string the beans,
up the storms and down the screens.

Pull the curtains, close the shutters.
Dreadfully the wild wind mutters.

Oil the snowshoes, stoke the fires.
Soon the roads are hopeless mires.

Mend the mittens, knit the sweaters,
bring my glasses, mail my letters.

Toast the muffins, brew the tea,
hot and sweet and good for me.
Bake me doughnuts, plain and frosted . . .

What, my dear? You feel exhausted?

Yes, these winters are severe!
Hurry, hurry —

Mary dear.

N. M. Bodecker

45

THE OWL AND THE PUSSY-CAT

The Owl and the Pussy-Cat went to sea
    In a beautiful pea-green boat,
They took some honey, and plenty of money,
    Wrapped up in a five-pound note.
The Owl looked up to the stars above,
    And sang to a small guitar,
"O lovely Pussy! O Pussy, my love,
    "What a beautiful Pussy you are,
        "You are,
        "You are!
    "What a beautiful Pussy you are!"

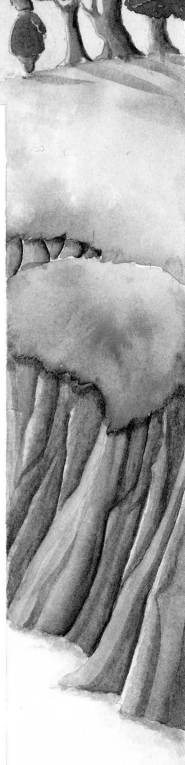

Pussy said to the Owl, "You elegant fowl!
    "How charmingly sweet you sing!
"O let us be married! too long we have tarried:
    "But what shall we do for a ring?"
They sailed away for a year and a day,
    To the land where the Bong-tree grows,
And there in a wood a Piggy-wig stood,
    With a ring at the end of his nose,
        His nose,
        His nose,
    With a ring at the end of his nose.

"Dear Pig, are you willing to sell for one shilling
    "Your ring?" Said the Piggy, "I will."
So they took it away, and were married next day
    By the Turkey who lives on the hill.
They dinèd on mince, and slices of quince,
    Which they ate with a runcible spoon;
And hand in hand, on the edge of the sand,
    They danced by the light of the moon,
        The moon,
        The moon,
    They danced by the light of the moon.

Edward Lear

THIS TOOTH

I jiggled it
    jaggled it
      jerked it.

I pushed
    and pulled
    and poked it.

But —

As soon as I stopped
and left it alone,
This tooth came out
on its very own!

Lee Bennett Hopkins

SOME SIGHTS SOMETIMES SEEN AND SELDOM SEEN

You don't have to go very far
To see a boat towed by a car;
But to see a car towed by a boat
Is *really* a matter of note.

To see a truck pulling a horse
In a van is a matter of course;
But to see a horse pulling a truck
In a van is *extremely* good luck.

William Cole

THE CHICKENS

Said the first little chicken,
    With a queer little squirm,
"I wish I could find
    A fat little worm."

Said the next little chicken,
    With an odd little shrug,
"I wish I could find
    A fat little slug."

Said the third little chicken,
    With a sharp little squeal,
"I wish I could find
    Some nice yellow meal."

Said the fourth little chicken,
    With a small sigh of grief,
"I wish I could find
    A little green leaf."

Said the fifth little chicken,
    With a faint little moan,
"I wish I could find
    A wee gravel stone."

"Now, see here," said the mother,
    From the green garden patch,
"If you want any breakfast,
    Just come here and scratch."

Anonymous

THE SWALLOWS

Nine swallows sat on a telephone wire:
'Teeter, teeter,' and then they were still,
all facing one way, with the sun like a fire
along their blue shoulders, and hot on each bill.
But they sat there so quietly, all of the nine,
that I almost forgot they were swallows at all.
They seemed more like clothespins left out on the line
when the wash is just dried, and the first raindrops fall.

Elizabeth Coatsworth

THE WOODPECKER

The woodpecker pecked out a little round hole
And made him a house in the telephone pole.

One day when I watched he poked out his head,
And he had on a hood and a collar of red.

When the streams of rain pour out of the sky,
And the sparkles of lightning go flashing by,

And the big, big wheels of thunder roll,
He can snuggle back in the telephone pole.

Elizabeth Maddox Roberts

LETTER TO BEE

Bee! I'm expecting you!
Was saying Yesterday
To Somebody you know
That you were due —

The Frogs got Home last Week —
Are settled, and at work —
Birds, mostly back —
The Clover warm and thick —

You'll get my Letter by
The seventeenth; Reply
Or better, be with me —
Yours, Fly.

Emily Dickinson

CATERPILLARS

What do caterpillars do?
Nothing much but chew and chew.

What do caterpillars know?
Nothing much but how to grow.

They just eat what by and by
will make them be a butterfly,

But that is more than I can do
however much I chew and chew.

Aileen Fisher

BUTTERFLY SONG

Butterfly, butterfly, butterfly, butterfly,
Oh, look, see it hovering among the flowers!
It is like a baby trying to walk and not knowing how to go.
The clouds sprinkle down the rain.

Acoma Indian song, translated by Frances Densmore

MOUSE DINNER

A mouse doesn't dine
on potatoes and beef . . .
he nibbles the seeds
from a pod or a sheaf.

He catches a beetle
and then gives a brief
little wipe of his mouth
on a napkin of leaf.

Aileen Fisher

PLANS

When I grow up, I plan to keep
Eleven cats, and let them sleep
On any bedspread that they wish,
And feed them people's tuna fish.

Maxine Kumin

I WOULDN'T

There's a mouse house
In the hall wall
With a small door
By the hall floor
Where the fat cat
Sits all day,
Sits that way
All day
Every day
Just to say,
"Come out and play"
To the nice mice
In the mouse house
In the hall wall
With the small door
By the hall floor.

And do they
Come out and play
When the fat cat
Asks them to?

Well, would you?

John Ciardi

DOG'S SONG

Ants look up as I trot by
and see me passing through the sky.

Robert Wallace

THE OPEN DOOR

Out of the dark
to the sill of the door
lay the snow in a long
unruffled floor,
and the lamplight fell
narrow and thin,
a carpet unrolled
for the cat to walk in.
Slowly, smoothly,
black as the night,
with paws unseen
(white upon white)
like a queen who walks
down a corridor
the black cat paced
that cold smooth floor,
and left behind her,
bead upon bead,
the track of small feet
like dark fern seed.

Elizabeth Coatsworth

CATS AND DOGS

Some like cats, and some like dogs,
and both of course are nice
if cats and dogs are what you want
—but I myself like mice.

For dogs chase cats, and cats chase rats
—I guess they think it's fun.
I like my mouse the most because
he won't chase anyone.

N. M. Bodecker

CAT

The black cat yawns,
Opens her jaws,
Stretches her legs,
And shows her claws.

Then she gets up
And stands on four
Long stiff legs
And yawns some more.

She shows her sharp teeth,
She stretches her lip,
Her slice of a tongue
Turns up at the tip.

Lifting herself
On her delicate toes,
She arches her back
As high as it goes.

She lets herself down
With particular care,
And pads away
With her tail in the air.

Mary Britton Miller

THE COW

The friendly cow all red and white,
    I love with all my heart:
She gives me cream with all her might,
    To eat with apple-tart.

She wanders lowing here and there,
    And yet she cannot stray,
All in the pleasant open air,
    The pleasant light of day.

And blown by all the winds that pass
    And wet with all the showers,
She walks among the meadow grass
    And eats the meadow flowers.

Robert Louis Stevenson

THE PASTURE

I'm going out to clean the pasture spring;
I'll only stop to rake the leaves away
(And wait to watch the water clear, I may):
I sha'n't be gone long. — You come too.

I'm going out to fetch the little calf
That's standing by the mother. It's so young
It totters when she licks it with her tongue.
I sha'n't be gone long. — You come too.

Robert Frost

THE FOUR HORSES

White Rose is a quiet horse
    For a lady to ride,
Jog-trotting on the high road
    Or through the countryside.

Grey Wolf is a hunter
    All muscle and fire;
Day long he will gallop
    And not tumble or tire.

Black Magic's a race-horse;
    She is gone like a ghost,
With the wind in her mane
    To whirl past the post.

But munching his fill
    In a field of green clover
Stands Brownie the cart-horse,
    Whose labor is over.

James Reeves

HOW TO TELL A CAMEL

The **D**romedary has one hump,

The **B**actrian has two.

It's easy to forget this rule,

So here is what to do.

Roll the first initial over

On its flat behind:

The **DB**actrian is different from

The **DB**romedary kind.

J. Patrick Lewis

PETE AT THE ZOO

I wonder if the elephant
Is lonely in his stall
When all the boys and girls are gone
And there's no shout at all,
And there's no one to stamp before,
No one to note his might.
Does he hunch up, as I do,
Against the dark of night?

Gwendolyn Brooks

THE WAPITI

There goes the Wapiti,
Hippety-hoppity!

Ogden Nash

56

POLAR BEAR

The Polar Bear never makes his bed;
He sleeps on a cake of ice instead.
He has no blanket, no quilt, no sheet
Except the rain and snow and sleet.
He drifts about on a white ice floe
While cold winds howl and blizzards blow
And the temperature drops to forty below.
The Polar Bear never makes his bed;
The blanket he pulls up over his head
Is lined with soft and feathery snow.
If ever he rose and turned on the light,
He would find a world of bathtub white,
And icebergs floating through the night.

William Jay Smith

THE WOLF

When the pale moon hides and the wild wind wails,
And over the tree-tops the nighthawk sails,
The gray wolf sits on the world's far rim,
And howls: and it seems to comfort him.

The wolf is a lonely soul, you see,
No beast in the wood, nor bird in the tree,
But shuns his path; in the windy gloom
They give him plenty, and plenty of room.

So he sits with his long, lean face to the sky
Watching the ragged clouds go by.
There in the night, alone, apart,
Singing the song of his lone, wild heart.

Far away, on the world's dark rim
He howls, and it seems to comfort him.

Georgia Roberts Durston

RHYMES AND SONGS

VIOLETS, DAFFODILS

Violets, daffodils,
Roses and thorn
Were all in the garden
Before you were born.

Daffodils, violets,
Green thorn and roses
Your grandchildren's children
Will hold to their noses.

Elizabeth Coatsworth

FERRY ME ACROSS THE WATER

"Ferry me across the water,
        Do, boatman, do."
"If you've a penny in your purse
        I'll ferry you."

"I have a penny in my purse,
        And my eyes are blue;
So ferry me across the water,
        Do, boatman, do!"

"Step into my ferry-boat,
        Be they black or blue,
And for the penny in your purse
        I'll ferry you."

Christina Rossetti

SUKY YOU SHALL BE MY WIFE

Suky you shall be my wife,
        And I'll tell you why;
I have got a little pig,
        And you have got a sty;
I have got a dun cow,
        And you can make good cheese,
Suky will you have me?
        Say yes, if you please.

Anonymous

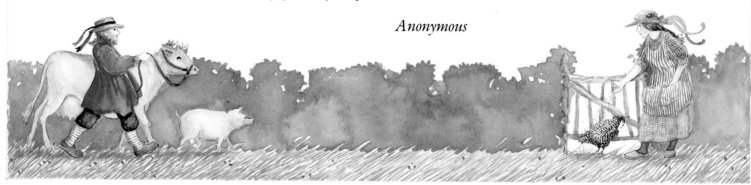

QUEEN, QUEEN CAROLINE

Queen, Queen Caroline,
Dipped her hair in turpentine;
Turpentine made it shine,
Queen, Queen Caroline.

Anonymous

SAM, SAM, THE BUTCHER MAN

Sam, Sam, the butcher man,
Washed his face in a frying pan,
Combed his hair with a wagon wheel,
And died with a toothache in his heel.

Anonymous

THE MOUSE'S LULLABY

Oh, rock-a-by, baby mouse, rock-a-by, so!
When baby's asleep to the baker's I'll go,
And while he's not looking I'll pop from a hole,
And bring to my baby a fresh penny roll.

Palmer Cox

I WENT DOWNTOWN

I went downtown
To see Mrs. Brown.

She gave me a nickel
To buy a pickle,

The pickle was sour,
She gave me a flower,

The flower was dead,
She gave me a thread,

The thread was thin,
She gave me a pin,

The pin was sharp,
She gave me a harp,

She gave me a harp
And the harp began to sing —

*Minnie and a minnie
And a ha ha ha!*

Anonymous

THE BLUES

When the shoe strings break
On *both* your shoes
And you're in a hurry —
That's the blues.

When you go to buy a candy bar
And you've lost the dime you had —
Slipped through a hole in your pocket somewhere —
That's the blues, too, *and bad!*

Langston Hughes

62

DICKERY DEAN

"What's the matter
    With Dickery Dean?
He jumped right into
    The washing machine!"

"Nothing's the matter
    With Dickery Dean —
He dove in dirty,
    And he jumped out clean!"

Dennis Lee

OLD JOE JONES

Old Joe Jones and his old dog Bones,
Go jigglety-joggle over the stones;
He sells meat-pies and fishery-fries;
"Heat 'em and eat 'em!" all day he cries.
If we don't buy them, he moans and groans,
Old Joe Jones and his old dog Bones.

Laura E. Richards

WHISKERS MEETS POLLY

Razzle Dazzle!
    She's so fine!
All dressed up
    Like a diamond mine!

So much glass!
    So much glitter!
Bright red dress
    That doesn't fit her!

Michael Stillman

PAPER OF PINS

O miss, I'll give you a paper of pins
And that's the way my love begins,
    If you will marry, marry, marry,
    If you will marry me.

I'll not accept your paper of pins
If that's the way your love begins,
    For I won't marry, marry, marry,
    I won't marry you.

O miss, I'll give you an easy-chair
To sit in and comb your long gold hair.

O miss, I'll give you a red silk gown
With laces hanging all around.

O miss, I'll give you a little gold bell
To ring for the doctor when you're not well.

O miss, I'll give you a silver spoon
To feed your baby in the afternoon.

O miss, I'll give you the key to my heart
That we may lock and never part,

And I'll give you the key to my money-chest
That you may have money at your request.

I'll accept the key to your money-chest
That I may have money at my request
    And I will marry, marry, marry,
    I will marry you.

Aha! I see! My money is all
You care about, not me at all!
    Well, I won't marry, marry, marry,
    I won't marry you!

Anonymous

JOHN'S SONG

It's a long walk in the dark
on the blind side of the moon
and it's a long day without water
when the river's gone
and it's hard listening to no voice
when you're all alone

so take a hundred lighted candles with you
when you walk on the moon
and quickly quickly tie a knot in the river
before the water's gone
and listen for my voice, if for no other
when you're all alone

Joan Aiken

THE WITCHES' RIDE

Over the hills
Where the edge of the light
Deepens and darkens
To ebony night,
Narrow hats high
Above yellow bead eyes,
The tatter-haired witches
Ride through the skies.
Over the seas
Where the flat fishes sleep
Wrapped in the slap of the slippery deep,
Over the peaks
Where the black trees are bare,
Where boney birds quiver
They glide through the air.
Silently humming
A horrible tune,
They sweep through the stillness
To sit on the moon.

Karla Kuskin

OLD MAN OCEAN

Old Man Ocean, how do you pound
Smooth glass, rough stones round?
>*Time and the tide and the wild waves rolling*
>*Night and the wind and the long gray dawn.*

Old Man Ocean, what do you tell,
What do you sing in the empty shell?
>*Fog and the storm and the long bell tolling,*
>*Bones in the deep and the brave men gone.*

Russell Hoban

THE COAT

I patched my coat with sunlight.
It lasted for a day.
I patched my coat with moonlight,
But the lining came away.
I patched my coat with lightning
And it flew off in the storm.
I patched my coat with darkness:
That coat has kept me warm.

Dennis Lee

ON A COLD AUTUMN DAY

Supposing all the things on the playground
flew away for the winter?
First the swings,
then the seesaw,
pumping its heavy wings,
the slide, turned over
on its side,
flying in a *vee*.
After a run
and a jump,
the long-legged bars
would go sailing by,
and finally,
the merry-go-round,
spinning wheels of silver
across the sky.

Bonnie Nims

68

THE GOBLIN

There's a goblin as green
As a goblin can be
Who is sitting outside
And is waiting for me.
When he knocked on my door
And said softly, "Come play!"
I answered, "No thank you,
Now please, go away!"

Jack Prelutsky

NO ONE

In this room
there's not a
breeze.

No one sneezed
the littlest
sneeze.

No one wheezed
the faintest
wheeze.

The door's shut
tight
with a big brass
handle.

Who?
WHO
BLEW OUT THE CANDLE?

Lilian Moore

SOME ONE

Some one came knocking
    At my wee, small door;
Some one came knocking,
    I'm sure — sure — sure;
I listened, I opened,
    I looked to left and right,
But nought there was a-stirring
    In the still dark night;
Only the busy beetle
    Tap-tapping in the wall,
Only from the forest
    The screech-owl's call,
Only the cricket whistling
    While the dew drops fall,
So I know not who came knocking,
    At all, at all, at all.

Walter de la Mare

QUEEN NEFERTITI

Spin a coin, spin a coin,
  All fall down;
Queen Nefertiti
  Stalks through the town.

Over the pavements
  Her feet go clack.
Her legs are as tall
  As a chimney stack;

Her fingers flicker
  Like snakes in the air,
The walls split open
  At her green-eyed stare;

Her voice is thin
  As the ghosts of bees;
She will crumble your bones
  She will make your blood freeze.

Spin a coin, spin a coin,
  All fall down,
Queen Nefertiti
  Stalks through the town.

Anonymous

WHO HAS SEEN THE WIND?

Who has seen the wind?
Neither I nor you;
But when the leaves hang trembling
The wind is passing through.

Who has seen the wind?
Neither you nor I;
But when the trees bow down their heads
The wind is passing by.

Christina Rossetti

THE WIND HAS SUCH A RAINY SOUND

The wind has such a rainy sound
   Moaning through the town,
The sea has such a windy sound, —
   Will the ships go down?

The apples in the orchard
   Tumble from their tree. —
Oh will the ships go down, go down,
   In the windy sea?

Christina Rossetti

SPRINGTIME

in springtime the violets
grow in the sidewalk cracks
and the ants play furiously
at my gym-shoed toes
carrying off a half-eaten peanut
butter sandwich i had at lunch
and sometimes i crumble
my extra graham crackers
and on the rainy days i take off
my yellow space hat and splash
all the puddles on Pendry Street and not one
cold can catch me

Nikki Giovanni

WEATHER

Dot a dot dot   dot a dot dot
Spotting the windowpane.
Spack a spack speck   flick a flack fleck
Freckling the windowpane.

A spatter a scatter   a wet cat a clatter
A splatter a rumble outside.
Umbrella umbrella umbrella umbrella
Bumbershoot barrel of rain.

Slosh a galosh   slosh a galosh
Slither and slather and glide
A puddle a jump a puddle a jump
A puddle a jump puddle splosh
A juddle a pump a luddle a dump a
Puddmuddle jump in and slide!

Eve Merriam

SUMMER SHOWER

Window window window pane:
Let it let it let it rain
Drop by drop by drop by drop.

Run your rivers from the top
Zigzaggy down, like slow wet forks
Of lightning, so the slippery corks
Of bubbles float and overtake
Each other till three bubbles make
A kind of boat too fat to fit
The river. That's the end of it.
                Straight
                down
                it
                slides
                and
                with
                a
                splash
Is lost against the window sash.

Window window window pane:
Let it let it let it rain.

David McCord

SNOWMAN SNIFFLES

At winter's end
a snowman grows
a snowdrop
on his carrot nose,

a little, sad,
late-season sniff
dried by the spring
wind's handkerchief.

But day and night
the sniffles drop
like flower buds
— they never stop,

until you wake
and find one day
the cold, old man
has run away,

and winter's winds
that blow and pass
left drifts of snowdrops
in the grass,

reminding us:
where such things grow
a snowman sniffed
not long ago.

N. M. Bodecker

FIRST SNOWFLAKE

Snowflake,
snowflake,
blowing into town
like one, last,
summer's-end
dandelion down,
or a cold little
raindrop
in her winter nightgown.

N. M. Bodecker

CYNTHIA IN THE SNOW

It SUSHES.
It hushes
The loudness in the road.
It flitter-twitters,
And laughs away from me.
It laughs a lovely whiteness,
And whitely whirs away,
To be
Some otherwhere,
Still white as milk or shirts.
So beautiful it hurts.

Gwendolyn Brooks

WINTER MORNING

Winter is the king of showmen,
Turning tree stumps into snow men
And houses into birthday cakes
And spreading sugar over lakes.
Smooth and clean and frosty white,
The world looks good enough to bite.
That's the season to be young,
Catching snowflakes on your tongue.
Snow is snowy when it's snowing,
I'm sorry it's slushy when it's going.

Ogden Nash

IN THE FOG

Stand still.
The fog wraps you up
and no one can find you.

Walk.
The fog opens up
to let you through
and closes behind you.

Lilian Moore

APRIL
1

MARCH
31

MARCH
30

MARCH
29

CLOCK

This clock
Has stopped,
Some gear
Or spring
Gone wrong —
Too tight,
Or cracked,
Or choked
With dust;
A year
Has passed
Since last
It said
Ting ting
Or tick
Or tock.
Poor
Clock.

Valerie Worth

MARCH
28

MARCH
27

MARCH
26

GARDEN CALENDAR

When the dogstar is aglow
plant petunias in the snow.

When the snow begins to melt
wrap your hollyhocks in felt.

When the felt begins to bloom
pick the apples off your broom.

When the broom begins to wear
weed the turnips in your chair.

When the chair begins to rock
prune the snowdrops in your sock.

When the sock is full of holes
blame the whole thing on the moles.

When the moles inquire: "Why
pick on us?" say simply, "I

will instruct you how to grow
pink petunias in the snow."

N. M. Bodecker

SONG

Love is a green girl
Holding a rose
Alone in a garden
Where nobody goes.

Time is an old man
Everyone meets
On trolleys and ferries
And cobblestone streets.

Michael Stillman

THE MOUSE WHOSE NAME IS TIME

The Mouse whose name is Time
Is out of sound and sight.
He nibbles at the day
And nibbles at the night.

He nibbles at the summer
Till all of it is gone.
He nibbles at the seashore.
He nibbles at the moon.

Yet no man not a seer,
No woman not a sibyl
Can ever ever hear
Or see him nibble, nibble.

And whence or how he comes
And how or where he goes
Nobody dead remembers,
Nobody living knows.

Robert Francis

COMING AND GOING

The crows are cawing,
The cocks are crowing,
The roads are thawing,
The boys are bumming,
The winds are blowing,
The year is coming.

The jays are jawing,
The cows are lowing,
The trees are turning,
The saws are sawing,
The fires are burning,
The year is going.

Robert Francis

MARIE LUCILLE

That clock is ticking
Me away!
The me that only
Yesterday
Ate peanuts, jam and
Licorice
Is gone already.
And this is
'Cause nothing's putting
Back, each day,
The me that clock is
Ticking away.

Gwendolyn Brooks

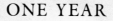

ONE YEAR

January played
a cold tin flute.

February sat
by the fire with a lute.

March was a penny whistle
sharp, cheap, clear.

April was a drummer
with a green bandolier.

May was a bird call
in the brave new wood.

June was a violin
that played as it should.

July was a French horn,
a hunt going past.

August was a hot-lipped
jazz-trumpet blast.

September was a zither
with a fine mellow string.

October was the woodwinds
waiting in the wing.

November was an oboe,
Plaintive and glum.

December was the boom
of the deep kettle drum.

N. M. Bodecker

THE EARLY MORNING

The moon on the one hand, the dawn on the other:
The moon is my sister, the dawn is my brother.
The moon on my left and the dawn on my right —
My brother, good morning; my sister, good night.

Hilaire Belloc

THE MOON

The moon has a face like the clock in the hall;
She shines on thieves on the garden wall,
On streets and fields and harbor quays,
And birdies asleep in the forks of the trees.

The squalling cat and the squeaking mouse,
The howling dog by the door of the house,
The bat that lies in bed at noon,
All love to be out by the light of the moon.

But all of the things that belong to the day
Cuddle to sleep to be out of her way;
And flowers and children close their eyes
Till up in the morning the sun shall rise.

Robert Louis Stevenson

YELLOW MAN, PURPLE MAN

Who is the East?
The Yellow Man
Who may be Purple if He can
That carries in the Sun.

Who is the West?
The Purple Man
Who may be Yellow if He can
That lets Him out again.

Emily Dickinson

TAKING TURNS

When sun goes home
behind the trees,
and locks her shutters tight —

then stars come out
with silver keys
to open up the night.

Norma Farber

THIS IS MY ROCK

This is my rock,
And here I run
To steal the secret of the sun;

This is my rock,
And here come I
Before the night has swept the sky;

This is my rock,
This is the place
I meet the evening face to face.

David McCord

THE DARK

It's always
dark
around my bed
and darkest
where I put my head;
and there are nights
when strange sounds
call
inside
the hollow
of the wall
and creaking noises
from inside
the closet
where
the
nightmares
hide;
so after I have said
my prayers
and hear them
talking from
downstairs,
I look around
so I can see
where everything
I know
should be —
especially
along the floor,
the crack of light
beneath the door.

Myra Cohn Livingston

RHYME FOR NIGHT

Dark is soft, like fur
Velvet, like a purr;
Lies warm, lies close
On fingers and toes

If dark cost much money
Rich men only
Would be able to pay
And rest them from day

If dark were not given
Each night from heaven
On field and town and park
Men would have to make dark

Dark is so warm, so deep
Without dark, how could we sleep?

Joan Aiken

84

MANHATTAN LULLABY

Now lighted windows climb the dark,
    The streets are dim with snow,
Like tireless beetles, amber-eyed,
    The creeping taxis go.
Cars roar through caverns made of steel,
    Shrill sounds the siren horn,
And people dance and die and wed —
    And boys like you are born.

Rachel Field

MANHATTAN LULLABY

Lulled by rumble, babble, beep,
let these little children sleep,
let these city girls and boys
dream a music in the noise,
hear a tune their city plucks
up from buses, up from trucks,
up from engines wailing *fire!*
up ten stories high, and higher,
up from hammers, rivets, drills,
up tall buildings, over sills,
up where city children sleep,
lulled by rumble, babble, beep.

Norma Farber

THE NIGHT

The night
   creeps in
   around my head
   and snuggles down
   upon the bed,
   and makes lace pictures
   on the wall
   but doesn't say a word at all.

Myra Cohn Livingston

YOU TOO LIE DOWN

Over every elm, the
   half-light hovers.
Down, you lie down too.
Through every shade of dusk, a hush
   impinges. Robins
settle to the nest; beneath, the deep earth
breathes, it
     breathes. You too lie
down, the drowsy room is
close and come to darkness.

           Hush, you
too can sleep at last. You

        too lie down.

Dennis Lee

LULLABY FOR SUZANNE

When she snoozes
Suzanne chooses
Leaves of willows
For her pillows.

Michael Stillman

SHEPHERD'S NIGHT COUNT

One ewe,
One ram,
Two sheep,
One lamb,
Three sheep,
One flock,
Four gates,
One lock,
Five folds,
One light,
Good dog,
Good night.

Jane Yolen

NO ONE HEARD HIM CALL

He went down to the woodshed
To put his bike away.
There was no moon. There were no stars.
He ran the whole dark way.
And when he hurried back again
The porch light had gone out!
He couldn't find the doorknob,
So then he gave a shout.

It wasn't very loud, though,
And no one heard him call.
He pounded with his knuckles;
Still no one came at all.
But then where he was standing
A *light* came streaming wide:
"My goodness, is that you?" she said.
And he was safe inside!

Dorothy Aldis

88

HUSH, LITTLE BABY

Hush, little baby, don't say a word.
Poppa's gonna buy you a mocking bird.

If that mocking bird don't sing,
Poppa's gonna buy you a diamond ring.

If that diamond ring turns brass,
Poppa's gonna buy you a looking-glass.

If that looking-glass gets broke,
Poppa's gonna buy you a billy goat.

If that billy goat runs away,
Poppa's gonna buy you a bale of hay.

If you grow up and get real tall
You'll be the prettiest baby of all.

Anonymous

THE COMING OF TEDDY BEARS

The air is quiet
  Round my bed.
The dark is drowsy
  In my head.
The sky's forgetting
  To be red,
And soon I'll be asleep.

A half a million
  Miles away
The silver stars
  Come out to play,
And comb their hair
  And that's OK
And soon I'll be asleep.

And teams of fuzzy
  Teddy bears
Are stumping slowly
  Up the stairs
To rock me in
  Their rocking chairs
And soon I'll be asleep.

The night is shining
  Round my head.
The room is snuggled
  In my bed.
Tomorrow I'll be
  Big they said
And soon I'll be asleep.

Dennis Lee

90

INDEX OF AUTHORS

INDEX OF TITLES

INTRODUCTION

DO IT YOURSELF? In the 20th century, we have come to
understand home improvement through this three-word
phrase. In our homes, there are always a range of
projects calling out for attention: a leaky faucet to be repaired, an
attic room to be converted into an extra bedroom, a bathroom
to be redecorated. Our decisions about which projects to take on,
and who should undertake them, are influenced by our dwellings
themselves, disposable time and money, level of skill, available supplies, and ultimately, our expectations about what a home is.
THIS BOOK AIMS TO PROVIDE a historical perspective on the fascination with home improvement in contemporary America. It places the
emergence of the do-it-yourself idea within the context of the early
20th century, when home ownership was on the rise, mass-circulation
magazines offered an expanding body of information about home
remodeling and repair, and manufacturers of building materials and
supplies began to cultivate a consumer market for their products.
Middle-class Americans developed a growing interest in home handi-
crafts. The experience of World War II encouraged this interest by
providing men and women with the skills and confidence to undertake
home-improvement projects on their own. After the war, economic
prosperity, the continued increase in the number of owner-occupied
homes, and suburbanization set the stage for do-it-yourself home
improvement to become a widespread middle-class phenomenon.
Manufacturers and retailers developed new products, marketing strate-
gies, and sales environments to appeal to amateur remodelers.
Changes in the design and packaging of tools, materials, and supplies
made it possible for homeowners to execute an increasing array of
repair, remodeling, and decorating tasks. The expanding do-it-yourself
marketplace transformed domestic life for many American families
and, in the process, became an arena to work out gender relationships
in the postwar era. In the 1970s, the historic-preservation movement
and a fascination with craftsmanship drew attention to the challenges
of restoring and renovating old houses. Do-it-yourself home improvement continued to change in response to new ideas about male
and female identity, as well as this new preoccupation with the past.
RATHER THAN ATTEMPT a definitive history of home improvement in
the 20th century, *Do It Yourself* seeks to open up the topic for
investigation and raise questions about why we choose to transform
our homes in the ways that we do. The book invites readers to

consider the complex interactions between homeowners, manufacturers, retailers, and the media that have shaped the domestic environment. By telling a story of how men and women responded to new types of houses and the products with which to repair, decorate, and enhance them, *Do It Yourself* illuminates relationships between architectural design, domestic life, consumer culture, and the history of technology. It is my hope that *Do It Yourself* will encourage students of these subjects to further explore the changing roles of specific products, how-to literature, hardware stores, and the many factors that shaped and continue to shape do-it-yourself home improvement.